The American Poetry Review/Honickman First Book Prize

The Honickman Foundation is dedicated to the support of projects that promote spiritual growth and creativity, education and social change. At the heart of the mission of the Honickman Foundation is the belief that creativity enriches contemporary society because the arts are powerful tools for enlightenment, equity and empowerment, and must be encouraged to effect social change as well as personal growth. A current focus is on the particular power of photography and poetry to reflect and interpret reality, and, hence, to illuminate all that is true.

The annual American Poetry Review/Honickman First Book Prize offers publication of a book of poems, a $3,000 award, and distribution by Copper Canyon Press through Consortium. Each year a distinguished poet is chosen to judge the prize and write an introduction to the winning book. The purpose of the prize is to encourage excellence in poetry, and to provide a wide readership for a deserving first book of poems. *Blue Colonial* is the ninth book in the series.

Winners of The American Poetry Review/Honickman
First Book Prize

BLUE COLONIAL

Blue Colonial

David Roderick

WINNER OF THE APR/HONICKMAN FIRST BOOK PRIZE

The American Poetry Review
Philadelphia

Distribution by Copper Canyon Press/Consortium.

Library of Congress Control Number: 2006924324

ISBN 0-9776395-0-9 (cloth, alk. paper)
ISBN 0-9776395-1-7 (pbk., alk. paper)

FIRST EDITION

Book design by Valerie Brewster

For my parents, David and Dorothy Roderick,
and for my sister Andrea.

ACKNOWLEDGMENTS

I am grateful to the editors of the following publications, in which these poems first appeared (sometimes in different forms and with different titles):

32 Poems: "Cod"

The Antioch Review: "Squanto"

The Bellingham Review: "The Point"

Blackbird: "Rothko's Earth & Green, 1955"

Boulevard: "William Bradford Drafting *Of Plimoth Plantation*"

The Florida Review: "Cordwood"

The Greensboro Review: "The Execution of John Billington"

Gulf Coast: "Bait & Switch"

The Hudson Review: "Priscilla Alden's Sickness"

The Massachusetts Review: "Excavation of the John Alden House"

Meridian: "Blue Colonial," "Into the Empty Woods"

The Missouri Review: "Colony," "The Good Newes From Plimoth"

New England Review: "Night in the Pawtuxet Woods"

New Orleans Review: "Oratory of the Little Way"

Ontario Review: "Edward Winslow's Cure for Massasoit," "The Indentured," "The Makers of the American Language," "Thanksgiving, 1621," "William Butten's Burial at Sea"

Phoebe: "Pawtuxet Hymn"

Pleiades: "Shadow-Casting the Billington River"

Slate: "Self-Portrait in 1969 (Summer)"

Southwest Review: "Catalogue for Prospective Planters"

TriQuarterly: "Notes on the Riverbank," "Waterfront"

Verse Daily: "Blue Colonial," "Cod"

The Virginia Quarterly Review: "Plot," "Thanksgiving"

Many thanks to the American Antiquarian Society and to the Gilman School in Baltimore for fellowships during which some of these poems were written. I would also like to thank my teachers and colleagues in the creative writing programs at the University of Massachusetts and Stanford University. I could not have finished this book without generous support from these institutions.

I am indebted to the following people for providing friendship, sustenance, and creative advice while I was writing this book: Rick Barot, Ben Beatie, Rob Bennett, Rebecca Black, Victoria Chang, Geri Doran, Keith Ekiss, Robin Ekiss, Louise Glück, Dorothy Hans, Tom Kealey, John "Trick Dog" Lundberg, Scott Nussbum, Rachel Richardson, Susan Steinberg, Meg Tipper, Mark Warburton, and C. Dale Young. Special thanks to Carrie Comer for use of the title "Blue Colonial," and to Elizabeth Scanlon for her editorial guidance and goodwill.

Finally, I would like to express my deep gratitude to Robert Pinsky for believing in this book.

After a still winter night I awoke with the impression that some question had been put to me, which I had been endeavoring in vain to answer in my sleep, as what--how--when--where?

HENRY DAVID THOREAU, *Walden*

Contents

Introduction

The past is difficult to know.

David Roderick engages that difficulty with precision and with a large, urgent definition of what we mean by "the past." History, and specifically the American past, has its sinister elements, as does personal memory: art at this ambitious level pursues those elements with the goal not of mere righteousness, but the higher, encompassing aim of truth. Even if the truth about the past is that so much of it is lost that we, its inheritors, become somewhat lost ourselves in what remains. The difficulty of knowledge is engaged, not erased.

Such is the terrain of Roderick's purposeful and extraordinary *Blue Colonial*. The title indicates a familiar type of suburban house, but under that denotative mildness "Colonial" also refers to the violent and beset colonists of Plymouth, Massachusetts, a body of individuals revealed here in fresh and unexpected ways, along with the native people they at first befriended and eventually displaced.

In the prefatory poem, the protagonist moves "through a whole century of second growth." Unseeing himself (navigating like "a mole" guided by sounds), he also moves "out of sight" — as if incorporated by those second growth woods that have "shaped the land and everything beneath it: / the incrops of rock, the wells bled dry."

The second growth woods, replacing farmland and wells laboriously created by the early settlers, recall Robert Frost's great poem "Directive," where the obliterating woods have swallowed roads, orchards, "be-lilaced cellar holes" and "two village cultures." Along with the second growth that reclaims the once-cultivated land, Roderick's evocation of blindness and invisibility also recall "Directive," with its invitation to "let a guide direct you / Who only has at heart your getting lost." Nature, like the past, is a dark realm where one must be "lost enough to find yourself."

Such a descent into the world of the lost is a poetic tradition and a New England tradition, and David Roderick is a worthy inheritor and extender of both. Thus, the first poem in the book proper describes an actual, literal excavation ("Excavation of the John Alden House"):

With cautious hands we pulled grist
from the past, turned space into negative space.

We needed a new language to weigh each item:
a pintle and fork, the lock of a snap-hance gun.

The knowledge that comes from this digging-down is not comfortably antiquarian, does not end with a quaint nomenclature, but with an estimation of loss, in a way enriched by the "negative space" of an informed bewilderment:

the dirt lulled us with empty spools, with half
of a cock's head hinge. The masonry was powder.

The artifacts, like knowledge of their names, are "lulling" because they give an illusion of completion, whereas knowledge of value is always out of reach, as the poem's closing lines affirm:

.... We thought we heard a murmur

from the earth, but the sound was a wasp nest
inside a skull. When our brushes found a delft tile
and wooden doll, a pin with an inlay of pearl,
we no longer knew the value of farthings or shells.

The macabre image of the skull with its murmur that is not a murmur and the innocent images of the toy and the ornament are equally effective: these are voices and signs that resist appraisal and insist on enigma.

That enigmatic life, exerting the powers of destruction and forgetting as well as the powers of survival and memory, sets a standard for the autobiographical poems in the volume. So one generation affirms its version of harsh New England realities, its rhythms of need and provision, harvest and depletion, in "Cordwood":

My father told me it was hard
to be a man, that every step
was either tentative or monstrous
and that God's dominion
was the smell of smoke in the air.

For smoke to rise from our chimney
we needed cordwood stacked
in the pitched shade of the trunks.
Our whole October was that.
The flames of treetops
were bright symbols of power.

But the next generation perceives those same rhythms differently:

My arms were heavy and I wasn't
listening to my father anymore.
I was trying to hear the difference
between each piece of wood,
feel autumn run through its grooves.

It is one of Roderick's distinctive strengths that the autobiographical and personal material is not neatly set off from the Colonial history. Nor are there only two categories, as this bold poem demonstrates:

THE MAKERS OF THE AMERICAN LANGUAGE

Strangers. Saints. Blazers of sphagnum and sap.

Trodden men with the land o'erturned on their crowns.

Oyster-shell plasterers. Shit shovelers.

Seed-sowing hands when the crabapple buds

grew as big as the balls of a bull.

Surveyors and tillers, pastors and thieves:

idle fools who were always whipt at school.

Soilers of lineage. White-whaling louts.

Wry tipsters with shillings sewn in their coats.

Criers. Anglers. Togglers of rough-hewn posts.

Cads who slept in ale halls and hookshops,

in the gray recess of the woods,

in dank stables of hay because they were

always such makers of contracts and rumors and wars.

The "cads" and "thieves" recall historical characters from Plimoth Plantation: the indentured, non-Puritan beer drinkers, the petty thief Edward Doty—and most surprising of all, John Billington, who becomes something like a surrogate ancestor, namesake of the book's "Billington River." These men were designated "Strangers," meaning colonists on the expedition to the New World who were not part of the religious community.

In "John Billington's Conversion," Billington prefers the Pawtuxet religion of Squanto to that of the colonists. (*Their Church is a Company./Shillings clink for the Saints.*) Billington's "wish to be an infidel" —a wish at the apparent beginning of an essential American tradition—has its culmination:

> I turn from ligature, buttons, boots.
> I burn my English twills.
> Squanto clads me in earthly fabrics.
> He tattoos my arm.
> He drapes my occiput with a feather.

In "The Execution of John Billington"—he was hanged for killing another man in a land dispute, Roderick's note tells us—the haunted and haunting narration includes the plural voice of the Puritan community:

> …. Brawn shocked from his head,
> black beard tangled, his sockets choked with blood.
>
> We almost left him hanging: a drunken rogue,
> a Stranger who worshipped water-dogs
>
> near the river that coursed through his art.

The shifting mixture of sympathy and judgment, the sharp physical details heightening the moral ambiguity, embody the originality of *Blue Colonial.*

The book is about time, not American history; or more precisely, it is about the intersection of time and knowledge, which I suppose could be one definition of "history." The group of poems titled as "Self-Portrait" with a date establishes the notion of personal history. "Self-Portrait in 1969 (Summer)" is pre-natal:

> The air will become me, and dirt
> drawn up the veins
> of the tomato vines will become me,
> and the mother-ovum,
> flowerless and hereditary,
> is staked to a post in the garden.

This figurative mixture of gardening and gestation, a kind of sublime comedy, is extended to insemination:

> The attic apartment on Standish Avenue
> is not blue, but the dappled yellow
> of a moon groaning
> through maple trees.
>
> The aftermath is two people breathing:
> the sweet sweat of humidity
> for the man
> but troubled for the woman
> who turned dirt to the light. 3×3.
> To popsicle sticks
> she taped tiny pictures of vegetables.
>
> If I become her son, which I will,
> if I become her last line,
> which I will, if I grow
> into her visible grief,
> which I will, I will,
> she can push me into mulch
> around mongrel trees
> or bury me in the beach-stone square.

Here is a poet's true evocation of time, of the fact that we all are destined to live in the puzzling, enticing tragi-comedy of our cultural and personal origins. David Roderick has imagined that destiny in a memorable new way.

— *Robert Pinsky*

Into the Empty Woods

he moves through dead-scrub and leaves,
between lindens stripped for winter.
Under the vaults of the creepers he moves,
and through a whole century of second growth
that shaped the land and everything beneath it:
the incrops of rock, the wells bled dry.
So much to lie down in. So much to cover
himself with as he moves out of sight,
as he walks back into a history that thrived
long before he had the legs to take him there,
the eyes to notice a moth on a limb
is a hologram, is a chute of light that bends
through the mind of a bird. Here is where
wings are hymnbooks, are precious gems.
And always the cones crunching under him
and his thoughts reaching past the salt licks,
always his head beneath boots of thunder
and lightning strikes. His eyes are closed
but he sees as a mole sees: diaphanous
bird calls, sounds to guide his blindness.
When rain strafes the canopies, he is involved
somehow with the ache they spread deepward.
Stiff and creaking, the trees are exhausted,
like rusted mobiles in the empty woods.
The sky surrounds it all like the inner dome
of a skull, and he stalls for a moment and waits
for the sight of a feather or leaf, for the random
flicks of the visible to break in on him sideways.

∼ PART I

Excavation of the John Alden House

We needed an alphabet to get our grid laid out.
Then we tore grass from the site and found
a pike-head, a spoon, a key with a hollow shank.
Voices behind us chipped into the ground,

our careful process of hunting, and then the ground
became an entrance to a room of cryptic scale.
The clays were tough but fill-soils gave with ease.
We found a bridle bit and hand-wrought nails,

a bell-metal blade with letters worn from its hilt.
The cellar bulged inward. Walls tilted in places.
With cautious hands we pulled grist
from the past, turned space into negative space.

We needed a new language to weigh each item:
a pintle and fork, the lock of a snap-hance gun.
The harder something was, the better chance
we had of finding it, yet the dirt saved a glass pane

and hoard of light, a written history of clouds.
We set up lines and sifting trays, ate lunch
beneath the plow zone. The chimney of stones
had been salvaged for something, but a trench

of ash remained. An Oak Tree sixpence fell
from a wall and relayed a human substance.
Then it owned us, that room, a museum
where other hands had slipped by chance:

a quill pen, a brass ring with the image of St. Peter
holding the key to Heaven. There was evidence

of water, of atmospheric weight. Ice divided
the ground, and though our alphabet was spent,

the dirt lulled us with empty spools, with half
of a cock's head hinge. The masonry was powder.
Some beams needed relief, so our backs provided it,
our shoulders. We thought we heard a murmur

from the earth, but the sound was a wasp nest
inside a skull. When our brushes found a delft tile
and wooden doll, a pin with an inlay of pearl,
we no longer knew the value of farthings or shells.

Self-Portrait in 1969 (Summer)

The air will become me, and dirt
drawn up the veins
of the tomato vines will become me,
and the mother-ovum,
flowerless and hereditary,
is staked to a post in the garden.

But a worm finds its way.
And the Japanese beetles,
even while carrying the weariness
of another day,
arrive and feast on the leaves.

Here is the father-seed
hunting for root, zygote, moss.
In each drill-and-sow spot,
each hole that is the beginning of darkness,
stars flare out into fingers.
Only insects feel the pulse
when they struggle
from grooves in the shingles.

The attic apartment on Standish Avenue
is not blue, but the dappled yellow
of a moon groaning
through maple trees.

The aftermath is two people breathing:
the sweet sweat of humidity
for the man
but troubled for the woman
who turned dirt to the light. 3 × 3.

To popsicle sticks
she taped tiny pictures of vegetables.

If I become her son, which I will,
if I become her last line,
which I will, if I grow
into her visible grief,
which I will, I will,
she can push me into mulch
around mongrel trees
or bury me in the beach-stone square.

The price, this year, is cheap
because I grow by the division
of the cell wall, and because beetles
haven't noticed me
reaching out from simple vines,
blood humming, umbilical.

Self-Portrait in 1969 (Fall)

Inside, a coil reaches
down to me,
bringing fat and grit
while dawn creeps over
my mother
again and again.
This is the void
that feeds me for months.
I am not
the star's acorn,
not the winter wren coming
to nest in a spine-bush.
I am the tickler's son,
the wolf's son.
Past is the moment
of illusion or choice.
While the house's shadow
smothers her garden,
I am the root
that cannot be
shoveled or burned
out with sticks.
The wall is both
ear and mouth,
where a voice tells me
the strongest is
most responsible. So kick
and heave. Kick, kick.
Outside, a radio
announces disasters:
floods, pestilence, war,
but inside I am

a safe inertia,
the size of a subject's
cut-out tongue.
Palimpsest. Footnote.
Seed of a tired world.
In the living room
where my mother sleeps
through each morning,
I do not sleep
because I cannot
yet imagine the still life
of her body:
stones and colored bottles
waiting for light to fall
through them.

William Bradford Drafting *Of Plimoth Plantation*

Once you adjust to the lack of light,
look at his map nailed
to a wall, lined with streets and plots.

Or the churn dash in a corner,
whey congealed
on its stub from the morning's work.

Near the hearth an iron skillet,
an unfinished pie.

And a woman asleep
under blankets and pelts,
the first sign of life in the room.

Then the bench
where William Bradford writes near a candle.
Tallow concentration. Glow.
A small jar of ink.
A goose quill dry in his hand.

Move in.
Look closely and you'll see breath
stream from his nostrils,
                                    closer
and his lips quivering
like the flame that lights his page.

Because this is the way history
was written back then.

A single draft inked near a candle.
And a wife warm in bed.
And mice too,
one needed to hear them running inside the walls.

Watch him stand and fumble
through his pockets.

The right hand holds a chart
of crop yields and births,
a box of wax, a company seal.

The left a scrap
of Wampanoag words
and a list of upright stones.

He hunts through these items,
mirthless, and walks out into the night,
where the moon taunts him
to embellish on past events.

Poor William Bradford, who knows nothing
about the imagination,
just a string of facts he can't quite recall.

Listen as the night whips
his beard and cloak, as he knocks
his pipe on a fencepost.

Bells. The drowsy baaaas of goats.

Listen to Bradford deal with the moon.

He draws in smoke and tries to clear his mind.
He stills a gate when it rattles in the wind.

The Good Newes from Plimoth

> Being thus arrived in a good harbor, and brought safe
> to land, they fell upon their knees and blessed the God
> of Heaven, who had brought them over the vast and
> furious ocean, and delivered them from all the perils
> and miseries thereof, again to set their feet on the firm
> and stable earth, their proper element.
>
> WILLIAM BRADFORD, *Of Plimoth Plantation*

I. LANDING

The right foot slips on a Rock
  but the left foot plants into sand,
  first steps of an infant
colony near a wrack-line of driftwood and kelp.
  Two shallops keel over the tide:
Strangers and Saints locking elbows in the froth.
  An ocean's fatigue.
A line of goodwives climbing the dune's spine.
  They have baskets or children
in their arms, iron pots, spools.
They walk toward hornpout and otter fat,
  toward the gleam of a minted name,
  but above them the sky
is spoiled cream, clabber from the bottom of a pail.

2. PATH

Down through the dark woods
into the chambers of His imagery,
marked snakes and creeping things,

wings that glide over
our path during cider season,
through this dark place

to the wooden chalice
and the pews of our dirt-swept meeting house,
see the candle of the Lord walking.

3. THE SECOND CROP

The sound from the woods was not the Lord
      or a cry from the Devil.
It came from men we saw through spyglasses.
         They stole from the trees
    and taught us strange plantings:
maize in black-soil, pockets of beans
      near our graves. They used the shoulder bones
of elk to cut the earth, crude tools
      that called for better skills.
We saw our breath and our horses' breath.
     We sowed through crow-talk
and laid out snares for the wolves.
      When each stalk reached
the size of a child's finger, we buried
     eels near its roots, then we nursed
the ground around it with beachwort and sand.

4. EDWARD DOTY'S CONFESSION

    I stole. A hucklebone. A spyglass lens. A scroll of costly paper.
Soon Bradford would know and lock me in stocks near the square. I
failed to ward off the Devil's voice. The spice of his fever burned
through my arm and hand. Next a small hatchet. Next a powder horn
from the cloak of Sam Fuller's son.

    With a pouch of bullets, I struck out to hunt for gamebirds.
For once the sun was not my master, not a rusted barrel hoop, not a
week's work at the stone boat. An hour was mine, then another hour,
until the shadows of afternoon clouds seemed to live around me.

5. ELIZABETH HOPKINS AND THE COLD SNAP

We feared for our lives when His drum sounded
halfway down the sky, so after combing the cribs
for last fall's leavings, we stewed some hay
and sucked on alewife bones. The standard
prayers held no sway. Our cord of wood
began to dwindle, and ice stenciled the faults
and cracks in our walls. We huddled together

even though we hardly knew each other:
wife and husband, thin children whose hair
had rarely been touched. My husband smelled
like pine-pitch, our daughters like straw-tick
and meat, but after His willing snow had wrecked
our field and our sins were finally cleansed,
the noses of our dogs were restless with new ideas.

6. EDWARD DOTY'S CONFESSION

Across the beach he was sprawled among shards and boats-chunk. The sun was a prod, and I reached down to touch his eyes. He had thick black hair on the backs of his hands. His head was scalped, but it looked like the work of a keel. His was a salt-swollen body, not yet corrupted by sea-flies, so I took a stick and drew a circle in the sand around him.

When the beach grew cold, I made fire with the flint I lifted off Winslow. I punished crabs and pentacles by dropping them into the cinders. Then I burned what I had stolen. Many useful things. A dram cup, a neck-cloth of buttons, the flint and a silver ring.

7. DOUBT

Where is He who gives us this beachrot,
these shells, this sandflat roved by gulls?

He is every sixth wave, the stillness after a tide-slack.

Where is He when ice moves from our handles
into our hands?

He is this frost with bits of blue in it.

Where is He who provides this salted wood?

He is the fire that empties the codfish of its secret.

Self-Portrait in 1970

Limbed Pisces, dawn of the Ram,
when my mother's hips
push me into lamplight and time.

This is where one voice ends
and another begins,
with a child bearing another child,

some low line
of election continuing,
a rabbit's foot stroked in a pocket.

Little cricket, little salt-boy
straddling two seasons,
making noise in a world

that already speaks so clearly of itself,
my pulse residual,
silence in my mother's spine.

The sky above the hospital
holds tight to its astrology,
the bowl of a womb scraped out.

Below, standing in the road,
my father doesn't know I'm born,
his horned son, a lungfish wriggling

into the language species.
It's a gripper of a night,
so cold his dental fillings ache.

Why won't he walk and warm himself?
Sober frostbite. Felon wind.
The road heading off in two directions.

Plot

The stones are grown over with moss,
canker-eaten, illegible even to the sun

leaving the outskirts of our land.
Cobbled fence. Property line that runs

into the pines, where my father taps a stake
in the ground, tacks an orange marker.

Pumpkins and mums form autumn,
and the next season prepares itself

like a spirit slipping into the skin of an animal
for some private need, to save a favorite son.

Soon there will be only two things left,
meaning and snow-meaning, bitter choices,

the kind my ancestors needed to warm themselves
when ice locked the doors of their cottages.

Now I see older things developing from my spot
at this window, like grass emptying light,

and the outline of a fox running along the far end
of our land, looking for something to kill.

Cordwood

My father told me it was hard
to be a man, that every step
was either tentative or monstrous
and that God's dominion
was the smell of smoke in the air.
For smoke to rise from our chimney
we needed cordwood stacked
in the pitched shade of the trunks.
Our whole October was that.
The flames of treetops
were bright symbols of power.
Their ashes fell to a river
where fish were faithful gestures.
My arms were heavy and I wasn't
listening to my father anymore.
I was trying to hear the difference
between each piece of wood,
feel autumn run through its grooves.

Waterfront

On the jetty I learned that each barnacle

had its own concerns, that the quietest gulls

were the least skilled when they fought

for french fries or bread. Sometimes I shared

my lunch with them, or I looked away

to a spit of land where the ocean used to be.

There was salt in my skin and in hulls

near the pier, in the iron cap of the Bug Light.

Bell-buoys needed a paint-job. The color

of beach-sand? Lighter than a boy's hair.

When boats returned with their catch,

I imagined the fog they had visited. I was

beginning to see the waves had something

to do with me. Some of the gulls wore masks.

William Butten's Burial at Sea

On the ship they wonder
how it feels to drop
into the ocean,
each second like a stone
in your pockets as you start
to descend, weight pulling
you to the deeper swells of the world.

You roll in seaweed,
drift on the folding wake.
Gray petals spread
on your ceiling of wind.

Light pours over your body,
and if you could swim,
you would rise to a place
where reflections of storm-clouds bend.

But here the weather is submerged.
Here fish stay calm
when birds cry for sea change.

Slow phrases of rain perish
in the water above you,
but you cannot hear
the sound of their passage,
or the wind that fills the ship
with new intentions:
sails ripped near the bowlines,
ropes that need to creak.

The sea draws you down,
but you will never reach bottom.
And you will never again hear
rats nesting in your sleep,
your mind rocking
in the hold, a swinging lantern
keeping time with the waves.

Your body falls toward
unending darkness.
Your weight is gone
and you seem to gesture elsewhere:
fingers pointing toward light,
hair in upward swells.

Time wheels in the sky
like a bird hunting for food.
Its wings circle over lingering
streaks of ocean.

Few things praise the body more,
and now the rain fades
like a hymn in the distance,
where children hold the railings,
and behind them men envy your descent.

Colony

First the sea came true
        and then the land because the bones
of their followers
found hard earth,
        foothold and roothold,
pine-pitch stains on their clothes.

        Clouds memorized them
and moved on,
        cool shadows pulled by a pagan wind.

        Because *every false doctrine*
stingeth like a viper,
        they built a gun-port and fort,
a row of lathed pews,
and when phlegm
        rattled in their preacher's chest,
they waited for another messenger,
        someone to write their names
        with a seagull's wing.

Why did they own this silence?
        What led them to this far place
where all the wrong animals lived?

Beneath the snow there were brambles
        and beneath the brambles clay,
        the hardest layer
they named for the English king.

Bareboned winters. Drenched hair.
Coins in the mouth of a fish.

All they wanted was a flawless green,
     a sky that smelled like rain,
something more sacred
     than a rabbit pelt nailed to a tree.

Catalogue for Prospective Planters

Two axes, a spade, a winter hearth that melts
a psalm for your tongue. Shovels of providence,
of spite. Hands where deposits collect in each joint,
gloves for a frigid spring. A mule trace. Refrains.
Lines in silt that trailed from a glacier's freight.
Dirt in the corners of the wheel-cart, the trough.
A son with a chin of stone, with a hint of hate
in his eyes as his forearms grow. Shovels of evidence,
of blight. Hope that a cloud will bootleg rain
to your field. An auger and some chains,
an hour of sunlight splitting your daughters' seeds.
Then seven weeks to leaven the shoots in your soil.
Vapored stalks. Aprons of handpicked beans.
This is what a sentence is: chance, two axes, a spade.

Edward Winslow's Cure for Massasoit

While squaws rubbed life into his limbs
and a powah invoked the charms of Hobbamock,

I looked among stumps and brambles
for some herbs that were parched by the wind.

I found nothing but chickweed and fleabane
which I chopped to a good relish,

and when the spirit of Hobbamock did not flush
the sachem's disease, I washed his face

and scraped his tongue with my finger.
This feat I achieved with the faith of birdflight

though it was fearsome to me,
not being accustomed to such favors.

When my tea passed his lips I knew
he would not starve or shudder his life away.

Men brought wampum, mowhacheis for my chain.
I made a woman bruise corn

and I took the flour and set it over grit in a pipkin,
and when the broth boiled I strained it

through my kerchief and poured him more than a pint.
After I swayed him to drink, he emerged

from the scourge of the low places.
His sight returned. His voice began to mend.

He pressed my hand and said *Ahheee Winsnow*
because he had no way to pronounce the English *l*.

The Makers of the American Language

Strangers. Saints. Blazers of sphagnum and sap.

Trodden men with the land o'erturned on their crowns.

Oyster-shell plasterers. Shit shovelers.

Seed-sowing hands when the crabapple buds

grew as big as the balls of a bull.

Surveyors and tillers, pastors and thieves:

idle fools who were always whipt at school.

Soilers of lineage. White-whaling louts.

Wry tipsters with shillings sewn in their coats.

Criers. Anglers. Togglers of rough-hewn posts.

Cads who slept in ale halls and hookshops,

in the gray recess of the woods,

in dank stables of hay because they were

always such makers of contracts and rumors and wars.

How I Learned Not to Speak

They were a hard and practical people,
 and when they said
 they were willing to serve me,
I took what they had to give:
 bowls of rain,
 prayer-husks filled with meat.

(Their firstborn, I.)

They cut my foreskin
 when heat was a prisoner in the ground.
The trees stood naked
 though the sun in Taurus rose.

When I chewed twigs for a change
 of texture,
 they said the scars
 on the trees were fire-marks,
that buds were sorry
from smoke
 and the far blood's branching.

I listened to them
 and grew: my hide, my legs,
the rhythm-and-rhythm
 of an animal glimpsed at dusk.

(I was silent but not still.)

Wearing a wreath
 of crocuses,
I walked the perimeter

because I liked
                    how the ground felt
under the soft pads of my feet.
        Wet with the night's rain,
                it reminded me of my gift:
a silence that was ingrown,
                        particular.

        Because they could do nothing
about the feeder flies,
                the nettles that bit my side,
        they did not like it
                        when I moved,

        they who planted the seedlings,
the small hooded flowers
        where I tried to sleep.

I received their permission
                        and their lies,
        and by guarding them,
be eating their brown bread,
                I thought I would move beyond
the fact of flesh.

(Strength in my muscles, my legs.
The sting in my side
        when I paced near the prickered fence.)

I kept my posture straight.
My mouth was wide and waiting.

Do you see?
                I too had desire,
but as befits a fallen world
                        I could not survive

unless I calmed them
              with my silence.

And so a childhood ended
                          and was buried:
        quiet lion, latent lute,
their hands reaching to touch me.

John Billington's Conversion

I. SQUANTO

From the top of a birch that leans over the river
you try to glimpse Squanto, that wayfarer
who squats at the bank and hunts the shallows for fish.

Or sometimes Squanto floats in a tide pool,
so quiet in his dislocation, where sleep
is the lazy spiel that spills into a language
you'd like to learn: *an nu ocke nippe*, nap in the water.

That's what you admire about the Wampanoag
language, how deer blood stains its verbs.

You, too, wish to be an infidel, to pry off
your boots and release to the river's persuasions,
so descend from your birch and make peace
with Squanto, that sagamore with a hummingbird
through each ear and a lynx pelt loose on his shoulder.

To wear such ornaments of feathers and skin.
To walk in moccasins of animal hide with ink
in your own skin: a nighthawk or bear,
a wolf stained blue in your shoulder.

Look at how Squanto cracks a squash or snares
a fish from the river. You want a bow and quiver
to strap over the muscles of your own back,
to hunt in the water with long reels of wampum
strung from your throat.
                Go. Be an infidel.
Descend into a new language and share
your gin with Squanto. Loll like a wolf near his fire.

I am no more an infidel than stars
that careen through darkness.

I am no more an infidel than owls
that swoop from their sleep.

My shack is perfumed with musk.
Fiddleheads curl from its walls.
I sleep under trees laced in fragrance,
the red pine and spruce.
I sleep on the twigs of the cedar.

I am bringing my body out of its old hymn.
I have no wants or extremities,
just to sing when queer thoughts enter me.
I sing to finches and jays,
to the bats that stunt after dusk.

When Squanto visits, we squat
beneath the Indian constellations.
The Nickesquaw mother
and her gourd filled with moonlight.
The Noei Comquocke
on a tight band of stars.
Squanto points to the wings of Ketan,
the good Wampanoag god.
His evil god has no name.

Their Church is a Company.
They fell trees.
They parcel the forest with fences.

The trees love my fire, their cuts
cauterized, diseases cleansed.
I break down the linden,

the oak struck in yellow light.
I whittle them down to kindlings.

What utterance from the sassafras cinders!
What untranslatable mouth,
with the curious power of heat!

Here prevail no laws but those
of nature, where blue quivers
in the larva on my bait-hook,
where the river drifts from the mist.
I sing to shoals of chivin and roach,
to flowers that tint into trout.

Look through this forest of windows.
The foxes lurk.
The water-dogs slide through the mud.
I am no more an infidel when I hunt for eggs,
when I bathe among the wand-willows.

Their Church is a Company.
Shillings clink for the Saints.

This land is neither primitive nor evil.
Look at the greenery, the moist leaves,
how the sun mounts the broad clear sky.

Cobwebs trail from my fingers.
Queer thoughts enter me.
I understand now how all history,
put to its terrestrial use, is mere history,
but put to the stars, becomes mythology.

I sing to mythology and magic.
I sing to the Wampanoag souls
that glint from silt in the river.

I turn from ligature, buttons, boots.
I burn my English twills.
Squanto clads me in earthly fabrics.
He tattoos my arm.
He drapes my occiput with a feather.

The Execution of John Billington

"He is a knave, and so will live and die."

WILLIAM BRADFORD

That was it: the rope pulling taut, his spine jerking.
Neck-burn, the end of the brilliant, breathing thing

that was his body. Brawn shocked from his head,
black beard tangled, his sockets choked with blood.

We almost left him hanging: a drunken rogue,
a Stranger who worshipped water-dogs

near the river that coursed through his art.
We almost left him hanging: his throat cut with weight,

his limbs stiff-quick: steles of rock, numb nerves.
His head was a green room, and then a grave

without a stone. To him, his body was a cloud.
His pulse: a trail of footprints entering the woods.

~ PART II

Self-Portrait in 1982

I was naked in the woods,
    shamed, listening for the noise that would make
me tremble.
    My body ached
    when mist entered the serpent
and spoke.

When I heard my name
    I thought a whole language
had died in the bones
of my ears:

flick-and-flick
    was the smallest sound in the machine.

    But I would come and become.
I would be the forked word,
    the dull weeds lunging
                against order.

Or I would become
    the subject itself,
my hand a root ball,
    the rain deep inside me
        as I began
my exodus into light.

To soil was to modify,
    so I was naked in the woods.
I was the rib of the rib,
    the tree's beginning and end.

After the serpent lost its legs
        and was perfectly marked,
a human hand
            reached for me.

It had mother-bones inside,
        but I left it empty
            because I could not return
to that humor:
        the earth's black bile, cold and gluttonous.

The ground was a door.
        And light didn't matter
because my body
            was coming into relief,
assuming its own shape, finally.

It was growing and assuming,
        growing and assuming.

The noise didn't own me anymore,
                  and then...

Blue Colonial

I was bored until I began rigging catastrophes: pitfalls,
tree snares, explosions. I dug a hole in the woods,
hoping that something would fall and snap a leg.

I shot at aerosol cans to burst the forest silence.
Shrapnel tore through ferns. Rodents fled along branches.
And the trees bored me because I'd climbed their gloom

to spy over our subdivision, rowed colonials, each the same
because a team of architects planned them that way:
decks too small for barbecue, monotonous shingles and brick.

Our colonial was the only blue one in the neighborhood,
a color I liked, but I wasn't allowed to paint it with my father
when it needed a fresh coat. He didn't trust me to brush

with caution and care, though he did let me watch while
he shot a squirrel with his BB gun one morning, a squirrel
that lived in our eaves. That's when I gave up asking

for chores around our house, my father at work in his mask,
sanding and priming rough spots, creaming a pail of trim.
Instead, I walked back to the woods and filled a hole

with my body, became a collector of hints and atmosphere.
I hunted for incidents, turtles that slipped from the surface,
feral slinks near the fringe. Once I found a pile of tires

in a ditch, but when I dragged out a pair, I couldn't find
a place for them, so I rolled them back to the mulch.
Those tires brimmed with water that only newts like,

and when I saw how the sun blinded their eyes, I stopped
meddling with tires and logs, vernal pools for the sleepers.
This was near Billington Pond, where a girl once fell

through the ice. She was trapped for an hour before her body
was pulled from its frozen zone. When her brain thawed,
she told about a vision she had, how everything she touched,

living or dead, spun into a string of light. I wanted to have
such a vision, to feel ice dazzle my eyes, a carboniferous
smell in my nose while I slept with the newts and salamanders.

The hole I'd dug held me still, like the hub of a bike wheel,
a trick that spins backwards. While inside, I was locked
in that girl's eyes, her irises crisscrossed with wings.

This is what I meant earlier when I said *catastrophe*:
some trick art, some careful recording of nighthawk quips.
I still like to visit those woods near the colonial

that is no longer blue. The subdivision changed
and is perpetually changing: living tulips sent into exile,
ivy crawling the chimneys. A pile of junk is a kind of faith:

rotten deadfalls, tires that sink, so I'll always go back
to visit the blue colonial and run my fingers over its paint,
knowing I lived inside it once, maybe three coats ago.

I look for depressions in the woods where I once dug holes
and climbed trees. I look for bike treads brailled
into the mud, an old thrill sculpting its chapter.

This is the place that keeps me frozen: temporary flowers,
dung-tinged fumes. I walk until I find remnants, shade,
a canopy for my sleep. I remember the trees by their shadows.

Shadow-Casting the Billington River

In early June the line-jerk and lip-tear,
breeze through pine roots,
    the waft of loam and mushrooms,
shimmy of the water snake,
    slit from gill to tail,
blue liver, pendulant heart.

Spit from a needle into our drifting blood.
    Spit from crawlspace
into the backtrack of rocks
    where midges and gnats are born.
See the design purling
    through that strange window:

    clouds like mud-painted stones,
clouds splitting over hills,
    breaking into thoughts and joining again.
Muscles in the taut shoulder,
    itch of the senses, five channels arching
into the tiny lacework of the mind.

Two slant-shadows
    cast across an embankment;
scythe-like names: yellow pike,
    pickerel, calico salmon,
still tines in the tidepool
    until the hook takes and line zips away.

    The pines in quiet breath-hues.
The beetles on fringed longlegs
    that quiver and twine on the surface.

The water snake, gaining shore,
        remembers the ground and enters it,
a tail wisping the dirt of a secret home.

The Point

The point is to roam out to the periphery
and return with something new to share:

a piece of honeycomb, a harvest of nuts,
the way the horizon hummed like a bass string.

You listen to bees prepare for a storm
and think there are a million ways to deal

with fear but only one conclusion to draw
before that storm scrolls over the cow fields:

some of the barns will collapse, while others
will hold and then fall in a future storm.

Nonetheless, you feel the rush
of walking into such a threatened world

and back again with a tune, or a yarn
to spin for others, even if the storm fades

from satellite shots, even if it fails to suck
juice from your power grid, your map

on a screen, where nothing stirs anew:
no pixilated colors that drift through the drafts,

no leaves that scrip streets like parchment.
You can fill your pockets with anything

if you walk before a storm: bronze nuts,
snippets of wire, strange pupae that warm

inside the lining of your jacket,
new momentum pushing your body

to rough-and-tumble harvests, stumped frogs,
newborn colonies that swarm over the cows.

Still, there's something necessary sheltered
in this language: words that are all sniggering echo,

meat encased in the shell, the space between
each word like a trench where frogs seal their eyes.

Perhaps an answer lies between those eyes,
two hatches, for there are always two hatches,

as in barns, as in wooded hutches built by chucks.
There's always a gist milking off another gist,

a storm hassling a hive, eye-quiet and back again,
tangling wires, tearing down lines to remind you

of something you knew long ago but can't quite recall
because you're still thinking about bees that seal

cracks by secreting wax from their bodies.
The more framework there is, the more lost purpose:

tape crossing the windowpanes, gummy cements,
cocoons that swing loose from their strings.

You lost your flashlight, which is good.
You listen to a candle flame hum in its wax.

Such weather is the best place to start
because it makes you remember past storms,

times when you melted the snow with your body
or picked through deadfalls while carrying

a shoebox filled with grass, your shelter
for a frog if you could trap one inside.

In your childhood days you were so merciful
when you noticed the blemishes in other beings:

the clipped swans that couldn't fly south,
the man who walked through the park with his head

resting on his shoulder, no neck muscles
you'd learned, some battle wound or surgical

slip-up that still seems to matter somehow.
You felt such compassion that your throat tingled

when he fed the swans and walked back to his mystery,
some obscure destination, a church perhaps.

And you also had no clue where you were headed.
You still don't, even while you walk under the trees,

but that's all right because the point is surprise,
the point is to roam out to the periphery

and return with something new to share:
some piece of history, a memory that squirms

from its gown and flexes its wings on your shoulder.
Like your hands milking a cow at a fairground.

You didn't know you could remember such a thing,
a cow that held still while you pinched her milk

into a pail, milk so white, udder so warm,
but you're too weary to remember more details

now that the scene has changed again:
barn with a cracked spine, hive on the ground,

a bit of sun rousing flies from the cow fields.
You'd think they'd move on, those flies,

but instead they bunch and sting the haunches of cows,
deposit their eggs in dung, millions of eggs,

another thing you'd never have imagined
if not for this silence as the wind finally calms down.

Bait & Switch

I recognize a bird by its shadow over the grass.
Perhaps a swatch of color lures it into the yard,
or actual prey, an insect caught bright on a leaf.

Everything I see is camouflaged: moth a torchlit
maze, pool a glove the sun slides into, one finger
at a time. The Mongols thought a fern seed

made its bearer invisible, and Genghis Khan kept
such a seed in his ring, but it failed to cloak him
from his lovers or foes. Instead, the seed helped

him interpret the language of birds. Once a finch
told him to conquer the land of Xi Xia, so he did.
That was the old world but still a world with its

own exterior logic: birdsongs, incessant pests,
maneuvers in the garden. All these hours I pick
tomatoes, bury kelp and fish-heads in the ground.

Maybe language will always be vestigial, a trail
of light in water. And rainfall an idiom. And birds
sermonic. I will be invisible here if I want to be,

among greenery and soil, where the compost burns.
I walk through my life like a king with a fern seed
under my tongue, beneath wings that shadow my body.

Rothko's Earth & Green, 1955

Perhaps each color was inspired by a sensation
in his pores, cigarette smoke in his nostrils
or the pleasant rise of heat around his head.
Red sweat. Ashen door. Then his whole night
was that: canvas and haze, the sour hint of dinner
still on his breath. Already he had left the room
by painting a portal into the next, and this despite
his urge to stay in this world, to frame an impossible
gesture. It is said he could not remember
the faces of his country: reading near the warmth
of his father's samovar, hide-and-seek in the crooked
alleys of Dvinsk, yet such an ordinary fear haunted
him in every green vibration and encroachment

of blue, every thin overlap the hue of rainwater,
every wall through which a trace of light might pass.
Sometimes a color was just the thrill of his skin
at the brink of discovery, like when a boy notices
figures in the grain of a kitchen table, or milk
swirling with tea while his mother irons laundry
just behind him. Corresponding signals of press
and steam, wisp and dispersal. And even while
painting he understood that somebody else must
open the space between them, that a viewer could
ease his passage by recognizing that his canvas
was a door to the common world, dawn between
then and now; so stare for a moment into the mouth
of this picture: inhalation exhalation, green
blue, the yawn of a man before he stirs awake.

In the Lining of My Father's Mouth

yellow meant forsythia
or scorched grass
and black meant mold on the foundation
or the leaves of the trash trees burned.
And brown was a post-hole proving something,
dirt that built character
while the sharp smell of foliage filled the air.

Thin and greening,
while seasons brushed through my hair,
I became sibling to the wheelbarrow,
brother to the axe.
I shook off my coat
while piles of leaves smoked around me.
Heat pinched the gristle of my ears.

But after many years
frost claimed my body,
and I learned I had to leave that place,
its umber pigments
and grunt-work,
where three tribes were torn
and continue to shiver
like horses, unblanketed, in the snow.
I learned the trembling
of a book, how hollows are put to use.

> Father of fathers.
Father-headlock and spare change.
In the grip
of spring, when pines smell green,
he plants coins to restore each summer.

And so I return, golden and drunk.
And so I speak to grass,
his wide lawn where the sun turns
our hair into wine.
Near the green forsythia
my father speaks
about human weight, hunger and flesh.

A man is just an illusion,
an ember shaken from a palm,
and so I return to that place
where my father and I
have been painted and released.
The mower and rake, the paint-cans, the gouge.
We consider them all
with the same-colored eyes.

Thanksgiving

For the heron that rousts the swamp, thank you.
And for spiders shocked into gradual sleep.
The rakes near the fence remind me to thank you
for balm. Thank you for ducks that tuck patterns
into various codes, because in the absence
of sunlight, the yard spades to a saturate brown.
Sometimes a song curls back down my throat.
Sometimes gourds rot or frail cocoons get torn
from the reeds. I hunt for paralyzed stances and nests
out here where the air is chilled with sly surprise.
Before the Billington crusts with frost
I gather river stones blotched with crystals.
Thank you for showing me how things grip inward:
choral frogs, sap that slows in its thermal sleeves.
No easy transitions, just recurring motifs,
warped wands that blend the species of wind.
When oaks molt their crowns, their colors spill
to my shoulders. Sometimes egg sacs burr
the fur of animals and fall into patchwork light.
Most of us hunker down for a while and sleep,
but some move around and listen for the hum
of a secondary life. I can hear it today, even back
in my garage, where all the sills are filled with flies.

Cod

We're off the headlands of a fable
where there are enough fish
to walk on, sea kicking whitecaps
around us but our feet dryshod,
our faces so pure we look oiled
by the horizon: Tropic of Cancer,
mer du nord, little fools glimmering
like shoes of light. Between
the cod's eyes is a flesh more flavorful
than its body, but we have no hunger.
We'll never have hunger again
because of this path we walk, each step
strangely warm through the leather
and steam of the krill-grounds.
There are whales deep below, blues
we'll never catch, and beneath
them there are cockles safe forever,
creatures that will never be served
with port wine poured over blankets,
nourishment that would go straight
to the center of our bones if
we weren't walking on this water,
if during the storm our sails held
from point to keel. And how satisfied
we'd be if we weren't dreaming
of wind behind us, weren't walking
on froth, this path of codfish
leading us out toward the deep.

The Indentured

In wooded places, mildly more wild,
indentured men drink beer in the warmth

of the pine trees. The forest's dinge owns them.
Pitch glues their hands and knots their hair.

The river is a heron's swoop in the corner
of an eye. Roots trap the bank. A musquash

drags a leafy twig in its mouth. *Hold on.*
Three needles: red pine. Five needles: white.

Days with little in them but scarred limbs.
Blue jay a sermon. Worms make proper peat.

Tiny yellow pebbles are sometimes seeds.

Thanksgiving, 1621

As seasoned birds drip from an iron spit,
　　the Wampanoag stuff apples into deer
And Massasoit opens his quillbox
　　for a cut of ottomaocke to pack his pipe.
Standing in the fields, children wait
　　for crows to descend, then they mock
And flap in a dance that sends
　　each flock back over the hillside.
Afterward, buzzed on the smells
　　of meat and sassafras smoke,
Boys realign for snap-the-whip,
　　and a servant hides a wooden doll
In a haystack for the girls to find
　　and dance among dishes of cream.
In a section of old forest, goodwives
　　walk toward the spring, buckets girdered
On their shoulders and more children
　　growing inside them, meekly concealed,
As if each wife balances what is hidden
　　with her need to hide it beneath a frock.
They whisper to each other about
　　the feathers in Massasoit's hair,
His painted thighs, the blue wisp
　　from his pipe. He drinks sap straight
From the root. His hair is sleek and long.
　　Behind him crabs roast on the fire's lip
And askoot-aquashes simmer
　　in pulp and seeds. It is cold by the ocean.
Children run to the fire, breathless,
　　pieces of straw stuck to their jerkins
And matted hair, their collars loosened.
　　It is getting dark now in Plymouth.

Their cider is gone. Near the cinders
          men kneel in conference with Squanto
And wonder what God has in store
          for them beyond this plentiful year:
A bundle of arrows wrapped
          in a snake skin, savage disease,
A killing frost that would require
          bringing the goats into their kitchens.
Thanks-be-to-God for the salted cod
          in our storehouse, victuals and beer,
Jars of berries picked from the marshes.
          Thanks-be-to-God for these racks of deer,
The blessed gift of Massasoit, our friend.

Priscilla Alden's Sickness

Snow came to us then, and I was content to die
under queer clouds that burned over the fort.
The spades seemed to multiply, leaning everywhere:

against fences and coops, even against pews,
and their handles were as long and terrifying
as the whoops we sometimes took for tribal men,

but they were nothing, just shapes in the sassafras trees.
Such strange visions appeared during my delirium,
beach demons with claws, odd quadrupeds,

wings that staggered through dusk. And the clouds
always flowed above these creatures atlantically,
glowing with a fire that burned my forehead

and seared my feet with frost, and these clouds
were so astonishing I tried to draw them
in my skin with a lancet. But then a worm pulled

the disease from my body, and tea took my thirst,
and the loyal blankets warmed me on the cottage floor,
and on the morning of the seventh day I became myself

again and bent over the hearth while my husband's body
twisted with illness. My wrists were thin and cold
but I endured them because I could hear axes chopping ice,

could hear Peregrine White shrieking from his cradle,
and because of this cold and sickness I knew we were part
of a land that meant nothing and would mean nothing

until the trees were cut and stones rolled into walls,
until our goats grazed and yielded firkins of cream,
and I felt, even through the cold that burned my fingers,

that by loving this place I might also love myself,
pour my pains into the river near Burying Hill
then watch them swirl and pull down toward the sea.

Notes on the Riverbank

Light opens the mind of the forest.
What took me so long to find it?

Jingle-flies on the compost pile,
a punched-in face of a pumpkin.

At this casting hole,
where the ground is worn

by rain, I smell local dawn,
a yeasty scent, vinegar the son

of wine. Near my feet a rifle
shell placed on a stump, newborn

spiders breaking from
a cracked pod. Sun stirs out

from the Billington. In its bed
I see pulverized rock, the gray-

and-white shape of a pickerel.
The marks along its sides

are like spots on an old man's lung.
I watch this fish, its stillness,

these toads emerging from camouflage
because I've found another language

to live in, where leftover light
finds my blood, and tree bark

is the color of dark bread rising.

Night in the Pawtuxet Woods

What I found was that my walk into Pawtuxet
did not occur to somebody else but to me.
I was no longer a Stranger among Saints.
I was an entity of darkness and movement
between trees. Autumn trees. Night trees.
Trees from which the blue gowns of bats
billowed down through the hollows. I listened
to the sounds the river made at night:
lingering, dreaming, trickling the path
of least resistance. In the fallen leaves
I heard creatures hunting or fleeing or both.
The ferns were brittle against my shoulders,
my beard. I crept toward a scent of woodsmoke
and found the oldest light centered in a clearing,
light that knew how to assemble bodies
and hunting bows, the pelts drying on branches.

Oratory of the Little Way

To row toward the lone beach,
then and now, to a new town
growing not only in my mind.
To stand on a rock and find
where the sand meets the oak trees
and lead my mare up the shore,
the C C C of her hoofprints
fading under dull-rolling surf.
To walk into the woods as silent as an Indian
and listen to a river's mild accent
and see three otters sled down the mud
into the great shad-feast of spring.

There was always too much Plymouth.
So much that trees began to fall
into the armfuls of their own shadows.
So much that the congregation
could not harness its silence,
a hollow drone that leaked into town
through cracks in the meetinghouse walls.
The earth-fast homes were packed
with a moss that blocked all slit-light,
and beyond Cole's Hill, where a statue
now stands under white shoulders of snow,
the meridian drew back to its new arc.

Here is John Billington, cloaked in gin
and tracking the river until sleep waylays his eyes.
He wakes near the otters' play
and stays to learn a tempo from the woods:
the fern-by-fern construction of its own language,
a hint that so much hinges

upon the thistles' hymn and call.
But even here there is too much Plymouth:
walls and stone chimneys rising on the hills,
a grist mill's wheel culling water
from mammals and geese,
a small fright-sting caught in their lungs.

I want to huddle down in the sinkhole
foundation of the Alden House,
to poke among its relics and make
a still life with the sipping gourds
and clay shards, a goat skull,
some arrowheads and beads.
I might find a trinket locked
in the ground, a pocket watch
dull and stalled with grit,
a charm to hang around my neck
and maybe thwart the hands of time.

When I ride into town, where the hill
is crowned with tombstones,
tablets from which squirrels leap into trees,
I hear John Billington addressing his congregation,
sharing an oratory of the little way
called "The Dream-Play of Water-Dogs,"
which he dedicates to Saints and the King
and those who force themselves into chores.
But too much of Plymouth disappears to hear,
so many fences aslant on the landscape
that the Wampanoags pack their homes
on their backs to settle deeper in the woods.

No wigwams near the river. No herring run.
The land has surrendered
to blueprints pinned to well-lit drafting tables:
the monarch-field scorched,
the bee-range engulfed,

the summer nights drawn off
by jet lights and transceivers.
Thus it is time to wade among eels
that look like knife blades in the river,
to pull the sticks away from my boat
and row back to a ship ancient in the sea,
where I will be but a speck in a bronze eye:

Massasoit, standing in the hilltop twilight,
holds his pose until I disappear.
Once I am through with my vanishing
and he has blinked for a moment and stared,
he will walk back to the river of the Great Time Before,
before my mind came and tried to arrange
all the things that were already together.

Notes

PART I

"Excavation of the John Alden House" owes a debt to *Pilgrim John Alden's Progress: Archaeological Excavations in Duxbury*, by Roland Wells Robbins and Evan Jones, (Plymouth, MA: The Pilgrim Society, 1969).

"William Bradford Drafting *Of Plimoth Plantation*": William Bradford was an original Mayflower passenger and the second governor of the Plymouth Colony (1627–1656). His *Of Plimoth Plantation* is the only first-hand account of the colony's history.

"The Good Newes from Plimoth": The colonists in Plymouth were split into two factions: "Saints," who were members of the Church, and "Strangers," who were not. Edward Doty and Elizabeth Hopkins were Mayflower passengers. Doty was an indentured servant.

"William Butten's Burial at Sea": According to Bradford, William Butten, a young servant, was the only member of the Mayflower clan who died on the voyage from England.

"Edward Winslow's Cure for Massasoit": Edward Winslow facilitated relations with the Wampanoag and allegedly healed Massasoit, sachem of the tribe and the colonists' ally in the region. Passages from Winslow's *The Good Newes from New England* inspired this poem.

"John Billington's Conversion": John Billington was a Stranger and signer of the Mayflower Compact. Squanto was the Pawtuxet tribesman who taught the colonists fishing and farming techniques. He also served as an intermediary between the colonists and the powerful Wampanoag tribe. A few elements from this poem were borrowed from *Mourt's Relation: A Journal of the Pilgrims at Plymouth* and various prose pieces written by Henry David Thoreau and Walt Whitman.

"John Billington's Execution": William Bradford sentenced Billington to death in 1630 for killing another man in a land dispute. He was the first British subject executed in the New World.

PART II

"Cod" was inspired by Mark Kurlansky's book by the same title.

"Priscilla Alden's Sickness": Priscilla Mullins married John Alden after arriving in Plymouth in 1620. In his poem "The Courtship of Myles Standish," Henry Wadsworth Longfellow imagines a love triangle between Mullins, Alden, and Myles Standish, though there is no historical evidence to support the myth. Peregrine White was the first English child born in the colony.

"Oratory of the Little Way": In 1921, a statue of Massasoit was erected on Cole's Hill in Plymouth. It bears the following inscription: *Great Sachem of The Wampanoags Protector and Preserver of the Pilgrims 1621 Erected by the Improved Order of Red Men as a Grateful Tribute.*